The Cumans: The History of the Medieval Turkic Nomads Who Fought the Mongols and Rus' in Eastern Europe

By Charles River Editors

The field of Igor Svyatoslavich's battle with the Cuman–Kipchaks, by Viktor Vasnetsov

Introduction

Ivan Bilibin's illustration of the Cumans fighting the Rus' in *The Tale of Igor's Campaign*

"Let us begin this narration, brethren,

from the old times of Vladimir to this present time of Igor,

who strengthened his mind with courage,

who quickened his heart with valor

and, thus imbued with martial spirit,

led his valiant regiments

against the Kuman land

in defense of the Russian land." – *The Tale of Igor's Campaign*

Before the Mongols rode across the steppes of Asia and Eastern Europe, the Cumans were a major military and cultural force that monarchs from China to Hungary and from Russia to the Byzantine Empire faced, often losing armies and cities in the process. The Cumans were a tribe of Turkic nomads who rode the steppes looking for plunder and riches, but they rarely stayed long after they got what they wanted.

From the late 9th century until the arrival of the Mongols in 1223, there was virtually nothing that could be done to stop the Cumans. Old Russian chronicles, Byzantine texts, Western European chronicles, and travel diaries of Islamic scholars all reveal that the Cumans were a threat to any kingdom in their path. Some kingdoms chose to fight the Cumans and often suffered heavy destruction, while others believed buying them off was the more reasonable course of action. The latter course often brought them into intimate contact with the most powerful kingdoms of medieval Eastern Europe before the Cumans were eventually replaced by the Mongols, with the remaining Cumans dispersing and integrating into various European and central Asian kingdoms in the 13th century. Many Cumans joined the Mongol Golden Horde and later became Muslims, while some helped found dynasties in Bulgaria, Hungary, and Romania.

The Cumans came from somewhat mysterious origins before they became the western vanguard of a massive nomadic horde that grew in ferocity and effectiveness as the centuries passed, but they were far more than mindless barbarians interested in violence alone. Although violence did play a major role in early Cuman culture, sources reveal they were also interested in diplomacy and eventually integrated with their sedentary neighbors. Archaeological discoveries further indicate that their culture was unique, complete with mythology and some art, but in the end, the Cumans disappeared as quickly as they appeared on the historical scene, much like other nomadic peoples before and after them.

The Cumans: The History of the Medieval Turkic Nomads Who Fought the Mongols and Rus' in Eastern Europe examines how the Cumans became a major fighting force in the region, and the influence they had. Along with pictures depicting important people, places, and events, you will learn about the Cumans.

The Cumans: The History of the Medieval Turkic Nomads Who Fought the Mongols and Rus' in Eastern Europe

About Charles River Editors

Introduction

Primary Sources

A Steppe Empire

The Cumans and the Rus'

Cuman Culture

The Cumans in Hungary and Byzantium

The Cumans and the Mongols

Cuman Integration

Online Resources

Further Reading

Free Books by Charles River Editors

Discounted Books by Charles River Editors

Primary Sources

One of the first major problems historians encounter when studying the Cumans is with the primary source material. Although there are plenty of primary source documents from the Middle Ages describing the Cumans and their activities, none of them were written by the Cumans themselves, and since the Cumans left no written records, modern scholars are forced to examine evidence left by people other than the Cumans, who were often fighting the very people writing about them. Not surprisingly, such works often have an anti-Cuman bias. Another problem presented by non-Cuman medieval sources is the nomenclature, as the people who had extensive contact with the Cumans knew them by different names.

The Russians in the city of Kiev, known as the Rus', were among the first people to record their dealings with the Cumans. In the Old East Slavic language history, commonly referred to today as *The Primary Russian Chronicle,* the Rus' referred to the Cumans as "Polovtsians" or "Polovcians" (Golden 1998, 186). The texts are pretty consistent with the use of the name Polovcian, so there is no confusion associated with multiple names.

Meanwhile, Muslim historians and travelers, both Arab and Persian, generally referred to the Cumans as "Kipchaks" (Golden 1998, 186), which was correct in a more general sense. As will be discussed later, the Cumans were part of a confederation of nomadic tribes including the Kipchaks, which is sometimes referred to as the Kipchak-Cuman confederacy, but medieval Islamic writers sometimes confused the Cumans with other Turkic steppe peoples, including the Pechenegs, who inhabited the region known as "Cumania" before the Cumans arrived. It is worth noting that Muslim writers recording their meetings with the Cumans usually did so under less violent circumstances than the Rus' and Western chroniclers, and they typically interacted with the Cumans later than the Europeans did.

Medieval Western and Latin writers knew them as the "Cumans," a term used extensively in Crusader chronicles and in the Latin language *Codex Cumanicus*, which was written by Roman Catholic missionaries in the 13th century. Western chroniclers also recorded the Cumans' extensive activities in southeastern Europe in the early 13th century, most notably during the Fourth Crusade. The word "cuman" was actually a Turkic word for "pale," as the Cumans were known to be fairer and blonder than the other Turkic nomads of the steppes during the period (Vásáry 2009, 5).

In addition to these written primary sources, the Cumans left some archaeological artifacts behind, usually funerary goods. Modern philologists have also conducted linguistic studies to trace the geographic and ethnic origins of the Cumans, although these studies are still open to debate.

A Steppe Empire

A major reason the Cumans were known by so many different names is because they were actually a part of a vast confederation of Turkic tribes. The nomadic Turkic tribes of the Middle Ages inhabited a swath of land stretching from what is known as Mongolia today to the northern shore of the Black Sea, and from Siberia down to central Asia. The land in this area, which is primarily steppe, is not good for settled agriculture, although it is conducive to a pastoral subsistence.

Thus, most of the steppe tribes of the era lived through conquest. Tribes would ride on horseback to raid sedentary kingdoms, take food, riches, and people, and usually leave as quickly as they arrived. At the same time, the tribes often battled each other for grazing and raiding territories, although they could be quite diplomatic and often made alliances. The Cumans hailed from one such alliance that at its peak comprised an area much larger than any empire before it.

Medieval Western chroniclers generally referred to the land of the Cumans as Cumania, but because no Western or Church official ever traveled extensively through all of Cumania, its true size remains somewhat of a mystery. It is known that Cumania's Eastern boundary was the Irtysh River in Siberia, and that at its peak, it extended west to the Danube River in southeastern Europe. The northern boundaries of Cumania were not as well-defined, but it reached ostensibly to the forests of the north. Since the Cumans' military effectiveness was largely dependent on their maneuverability and horsemanship, it is more than likely that the northern forests served as an effective barrier, and there were also no notable cities or settlements for the Cumans to pillage in the northern forests.

A map of Cumania

Cumania's southern boundaries were more clearly defined by natural barriers. The Black Sea, the Caucus Mountains, and Lake Balkhash all served more or less as the southern boundary of Cumania along the same latitude (Vásáry 2009, 7).

The confederacy that originally populated Cumania was known as the Kipchaks, who were originally a part of what were known as the "Six Sir Tribes" from the 6th-8th centuries CE. The Six Sir Tribes were headquartered on the Syr-darya River in what is now the modern nation of Kazakhstan (Klyashtornyj 2005, 243). As the Kipchaks and their allies became successful raiding the fringes of the Eastern steppes, they eventually became part of the Kimek Khanate (Golden 1998, 183).

By the 10th century, the Kipchak confederacy was already an ethnically mixed association, and it was quite large and growing. The Kipchaks controlled the steppes as far as the Volga River and regularly came into contact with Arab and Persian merchants and explorers. One of the most famous Islamic explorers to make contact with and write about the Kipchak confederation in the 10th century was Ibn Fadlān. He wrote the following about the allied Bāshghirids: "We set out again and stopped at the river Jāyikh which was the largest we had seen, the most impressive and the swiftest. I saw a leather boat overturned in midstream and those who were in it drowned. Many of our men were carried away and a certain number of horses and camels were drowned. It cost us great efforts to get across that river. Then we marched for several days and crossed the Jākhā, after which we cross[ed] the Arkhaz, then the Bājāgh, then the Samūr, then the Kināl, then the river Sūkh, and finally the river Kunjulū. Then we halted in the lands of a Turkic people, the Bāshghirds." (Fadlān 2010, 23)

The Kimek Khanate continued to grow, absorbing more and more people of the steppe until it incorporated the Cumans in the 11th century. The precise date and the circumstances under which the Cumans joined the Kimek confederacy are unknown, but based on what is known about Turkic nomadic tribes of the period, a basic outline can be drawn. The Cumans probably lived on the edge of the Kimek confederacy and were invited to join once their effectiveness as raiders and warriors was established. Around the same time, the nature of the Kimek Khanate had changed by the time the Cumans came on the scene because the Kipchaks had supplanted the Kimeks as the dominant tribe, so it essentially became the Kipchak confederation (Golden 1998, 184). The Cumans would become the western branch of the Kipchak confederation, and they eventually moved westward across nebulous Europe-Asia borders (Klyashtornyj 2005, 247).

The European peoples the Cumans encountered in the west were all sedentary. Moreover, many had enduring kingdoms, and most viewed the nomads as a threat, rightfully so. Still others learned to adapt to the Cuman presence in Eastern Europe, and a few would use the Cumans to their advantage.

The Cumans and the Rus'

The Rus' were one of the first European peoples the Cumans encountered. The "Viking Rus'," as they are sometimes known, were a Scandinavian tribe that historians believe originated in the central coastal area of modern Sweden. As with other Vikings, they set up trade routes around Europe, including the seas and waterways and stretching into Eurasia, dealing in furs, precious metals, and even slaves. What was particularly significant about the Vikings, including the Rus', was their ability and desire to set up colonies. The Vikings found success in the period after the fall of the Roman Empire, an era lasting centuries in which Europe descended into war and barbarity.[1] The Romans might have subjugated the continent, but they also made strides in terms of learning, science, literature, and so on. The Vikings, perhaps in a more circular fashion, also moved the people of Europe and Eurasia forward developmentally. This can be seen in the transformation of the Rus' from marauders to settlers, and eventually the standard-bearers of a new version of Christianity. Establishing a network of settlements, first through raids and then through trading, the Vikings' influence stretched far and wide across the continent. They were also known as feared, brutal warriors.

Along with their military prowess and skill at navigating the seas through their advanced ships, the Vikings also assimilated into local populations through marriage and by taking on the beliefs, languages, and customs of the individual regions in which they settled. The Scandinavian Vikings controlled the forests in the north of the region but failed to take full control of the steppe to the south. The Scandinavians were known as the Rus' by the locals, and they started converting to the Byzantine version of Christianity from the influence of southern Greeks. Rus' leaders took on Slavic names and intermarried with the local Slav population.[2]

By the mid-9th century, the Rus' lived on land to the north of modern Ukraine, in what is now BelaRus'. Kiev was taken from the Khazars by the Varangian (a synonym for Vikings) Army, led by Prince Oleg in 882, thus beginning the Kievan Rus' reign.

The Rus' then came into conflict with other powers in the region, including the Byzantines and Khazars. A number of peace treaties were signed, and an area began to form, including Ukraine. The territory dominated by the Kievan Rus' included modern-day Ukraine, BelaRus', parts of Russia, and stretched all the way up to Finland. Lasting until the middle of the 13th century, at its peak the Kievan Rus' spanned the land from the White Sea in the north to the Black Sea in the south. Established as a relatively loose configuration, perhaps best thought of as a federation of authorities and people, the Kievan Rus' based itself in Kiev and included the town of Novgorod.

Some historians have contested this version of the Rus' origins, with some believing they were descendants of the Slavic tribes and those believing they migrated from Scandinavia. The more

---

[1] Marr 2012
[2] Snyder 2016

conventional narrative describes Scandinavian Vikings settling in Kiev and the surrounding region and adopting the Slavic customs and language, all while integrating into the local population. In any case, it seems clear that Prince Oleg had assumed control of Kiev by 882 and used the city as the base for the Kievan Rus'. With this conquest, the Scandinavians essentially controlled river trade routes from the Baltic to the Black Sea and beyond.[3]

In the 11th century, the Rus' were led by Yaroslav the Wise from 1019-1054. Yaroslav built churches in the country and encouraged Kiev's development into an imperial capital. By the end of his reign, the Kievan Rus' territory stretched from the Black Sea to the Baltic Sea and as far west as the Carpathian Mountains.

This period is sometimes considered the "golden age" of the Kievan Rus', but the kingdom also began to disintegrate around the middle of the 11th century. This was due to a number of factors, including factionalism within the Kievan Rus'. The decline of Constantinople was also key to these developments, as the Rus' economy was dependent on the Byzantine capital's prosperity.

Still, it took a century of declining fortunes to weaken the Kievan Rus' enough that it was truly vulnerable to attack from outsiders. Kiev was sacked in 1169 by another Rus' faction and was sucked into the Crusades when Constantinople was attacked in 1204, further devastating the Rus' trade routes. Novgorod also stood apart from the Rus', declaring the Novgorod Republic in 1136. While Novgorod continued to prosper relative to its neighbors, Kiev split into 12 different component regions, which obviously strained everyone and everything involved.

Like their Viking ancestors, the Rus' were warlike and sometimes brutal, although they did not raid as much as their northern relatives and focused most of their non-martial energies on trade and diplomacy. Not long after arriving in Eastern Europe, the Vikings had mixed with the native Slavs, essentially creating the Rus' culture. The early Rus' princes then converted to Orthodox Christianity to make it a distinctly Eastern European culture.

The Rus' princes arranged diplomatic marriages between themselves and other monarchs in Eastern Europe and sometimes went to war, although their wars were usually over very quickly. There was a protocol that princes followed, but it was shattered when the Cumans arrived on the scene.

The Cumans first began to interact with the Rus' in 1054, when they arrived outside the gates of Kiev during Grand Prince Izyaslav's rule (lasting from 1054-1078, aside from two brief periods of time during which he was deposed). Izyaslav took power under precarious conditions, as his brothers, who ruled other Russian principalities, coveted Kiev, and he had seemingly few friends to help him. According to the *Russian Primary Chronicle*, the Cumans (Polovcians)

---

[3] Marr 2012

arrived outside of Kiev as the new grand price was attempting to stabilize the region: "Izyaslav then took up his abode in Kiev, with Svyatoslav in Chernigov, Vsevolod at Pereyaslavl', Igor' in Vladimir, and Vyacheslav at Smolensk. In this year, Vsevolod attacked the Torks during the winter near Voin' and conquered them. In the same year, Bolush advanced with his Polovcians, but Vsevolod made peace with them, and they returned whence they came." (Cross and Serbowitz-Wetzor 2012, 143).

The peace that Izyaslav's younger brother Vsevolod made with the Cumans did not last long, because the Cumans soon realized that Kiev was more than just another camp along the river. Once they determined Kiev was actually a place of riches, a new Cuman army advanced on it, but instead of being led by Bolush, a man named Iskal was their chief. The *Russian Primary Chronicle* explained, "The Polovcians invaded Rus' to make war for the first time. On February 2, Vsevolo went forth against them. When they met in battle, the Polovcians defeated Vesevolod, but after combat they retired. This was the first evil done by these [P]agan and godless foes. Their prince was Iskal. (Cross and Serbowitz-Wetzor 2012, 143). The Cumans may have been defeated this time, but they were far from done with the Rus'.

Besides the chronological information, the texts provide a glimpse into the nature of the Cuman government. Although the Cumans controlled a vast area, they were a decentralized people with many warlords or chieftains. The Russian principalities offered a wide range of opportunities to Cuman chieftains that could not be attained on the steppes, so they lingered outside of Kiev and other cities, waiting for an opening.

The Cumans did not have to wait long for another opportunity. By 1070, the Rus' became involved in a bloody civil war that spread anarchy throughout Russia, while the Cumans had become masters of the western steppe (Golden 1998, 186). Furthermore, the Cumans had already conquered the steppe around the north shore of the Black Sea by 1068, which meant that they controlled the routes between the Rus' and Byzantium (Font 2005, 269). By the mid-11th century, the Rus' were influenced just as much if not more by the Byzantine Empire to the south than they were by their Viking and Slavic ancestors. The Rus' were still powerful enough to resist the Cumans, and they continued to control the important Dnepr River route, which connected them to the Black Sea and the Byzantine Empire.

As Izyaslav and Vsevolod fought the other Rus' princes, the Cumans ravaged the land outside of Kiev, which turned the people of the city against the prince. The *Russian Primary Chronicle* continued, "When Izyaslav, accompanied by Vsevolod, had fled to Kiev, while Svyatoslav had taken refuge in Chernigov, the men of Kiev who had escaped to their native city held an assembly on the market place and sent the following communication to the Prince: 'The Polovcians have spread over the country. Oh[,] Prince, give us arms and horses, that we may offer them combat once more.' Izyaslav, however, paid no heed to this request…The mob then gave a shout and went off to Vselav's prison. When Izyaslav beheld their action, he fled with

Vsevolod from the palace…While the Polovians were ravaging throughout the land of Rus',
Svyatoslave was meanwhile at Chernigov. As soon as the [P]agans raided around Chernigov
itself, Svyatoslav collected a small force and sallied out against them to Snovsk. The Polovcians
remarked the approaching troops and marshalled their forces for resistance. When Svyatoslav
observed their numbers, he said to his followers, 'Let us attack, for it is too late for us to seek
succor elsewhere.' They spurred up their horses, and though the Polovcians had twelve thousand
men, Svyatoslav won the day with his force of only three thousand." (Cross and Serbowitz-
Wetzor 2012, 148-9). Although Izyaslav was temporarily deposed as a result of the situation, he
was able to return to power, ensuring that Vsevolod I (r. 1078-1093) would come to power.
Furthermore, all of the Rus' princes realized the Cumans were not going away anytime soon, and
that if need be, they could be used against the other princes.

Vsevolod I inherited the wealthiest and strongest of all Russian principalities from his brother,
but along with it came constant challenges from other Rus' princes and Cumans. The political
status quo hadn't changed much while Izyaslav was on the throne, aside from the fact the
Cumans began to play a larger role in the general political situation of the region at that time. At
the same time, however, the Rus' princes realized that the Cumans were more interested in
plundering Russia and returning to the steppes than they were in occupying any principalities.
The princes thus began enticing the Cumans with payments and promises of even more riches
when Kiev was ultimately plundered.

A 17th century depiction of Vsevolod I

Due to this situation, Vsevolod I spent most of his rule defending Kiev from the combined efforts of the other Rus' princes and the Cumans. The *Primary Russian Chronicle* noted that he lost many of his people in the fight: "While Svyatopolk, the son of Izyaslav, was ruling at Novgorod in his stead, and while Yaropolk was reigning in Vyshgorod and Vladimir at Smolensk, Oleg and Boris led the [P]agans to attack [the] Rus', and fell upon Vsevolod with their Polovcian reinforcements. Vsevolod advanced to meet them as far as the Sozhitsa. The Polovcians then vanquished the Russes, and many lost their lives. Ivan, son of Zhiroslav and Tuky, the brother of Chudin, along with Porey and many others, met their deaths there on August 28." (Cross and Serbowitz-Wetzor 2012, 165).

Vsevolod I did little to stop the Cumans, and by the time he died in 1093, they had raided

Russia with impunity. He was succeeded by Sviatopolk II (r. 1093-1113), an illegitimate son of Izyaslav, and according to the *Primary Russian Chronicle*, the Cumans were about to attack Kiev when they learned that Vsevolod had died. Showing that they could be just as diplomatic as they were bellicose, the Cumans sent envoys to the new grand prince to initiate peace, but instead of hearing out the Cuman envoys, Sviatopolk decided to put them in prison. The *Primary Russian Chronicle* explained, "At this moment, the Polovcians attacked Rus', but when they learned that Vsevolod was dead, they sent propositions for peace to Svyatopolk. Without consulting with the numerous adherents of his father and his uncle, but taking counsel only with those who had accompanied him to the capital, Svyatopolk seized the Polovcian envoys and cast them in prison. When the Polovcians heard of this outrage, they immediately declared war. A large force of them thus laid siege to the city of Torchesk. Being desirous of peace, Svyatopolk released the Polovcian envoys." (Cross and Serbowitz-Wetzor 2012, 175).

Alexey Danilovich Kivshenko's painting of Sviatopolk II

It is still unclear why Sviatopolk made such a drastic move. It could be that he wanted to send a message to the Cumans that he would be no pushover and that he was a different ruler than his predecessor, but there are other possibilities that could be considered. Perhaps Sviatopolk had received bad advice from his advisors, or maybe he simply acted brashly and without much forethought. Whatever the reason, Sviatopolk had a major problem on his hands when the Cumans raised a major force to invade Kiev.

Unlike his previous two predecessors, Sviatopolk was able to forge more effective alliances with other Rus' princes. When the Cuman horde came to Kiev seeking vengeance in 1093, Sviatopolk was able to meet them with an equally impressive Rus' army, but once again, the battle would be a disaster: "The Polovcians, however, were not anxious for peace, and continued their attacks. Svyatopolk then set out to recruit a force with the intention of attacking them. The wise men advised him not to oppose the nomads, since his force was small…After marshalling their troops, Svyatopolk, Vladimir, and Rostislav then moved forward. Svyatopolk marched on the right wing, Vladimir on the left, and Rostislav led the centre. When they had passed Trepol' they passed the rampart. Then the Polovcians advanced to the attack with their bowmen in the van. When our men took position between the ramparts they set up their standards, and the bowmen advanced outside the rampart. The Polvcians reached the rampart, raised their standards, and first attacked Svyatopolk, whose troop they broke up. Svyatopolk made a firm stand, but his soldiers fled without resisting the [P]agan onslaught, and he himself was obliged to flee also…Upon perceiving their victory, the Polovcians scattered upon marauding expeditions throughout the countryside, while others returned to Torchesk." (Cross and Serbowitz-Wetzor 2012, 175-6)

Some of the most interesting information gleaned from the passage concerns the Cumans' tactics. Cavalry archers were central to the Cuman military, playing a major role in all of their major battlefield victories, but what is maybe even more interesting is what the Cumans did after they won the battle: instead of staying to occupy the land they had just won, they broke into smaller groups and plundered the area before returning to their homeland. Contemporary sources documented the Cumans repeating this pattern several times across wide geographical distances and over the course of centuries.

Sviatopolk II's war against the Cumans ebbed and flowed, but it was at its most intense during the first few years of his reign. It seems the Cumans believed the new prince was weak and not up to the task of protecting Kiev from them and the other Rus' princes. A Cuman chieftain named Bonjak was particularly effective in his raids against Kiev, making his way into the city and destroying many holy Orthodox Christian monuments in the process. According to the *Primary Russian Chronicle*, "At this time, Bonyak and his Polovcians appeared before Kiev on a Sunday evening, and while ravaging the environs, they burned the prince's palace at Berestovo. Kurya and another band of Polovcians ravaged simultaneously the environs of Pereyaslavl', and burned Us'e on May 24…On Friday, the twentieth of this same month, Bonyak, that godless, mangy thief and bandit, came suddenly to Kiev for the second time. The Polovcians almost entered the city, burned the suburbs about the town, and then attacked the monastery…Then they burned the red palace which the pious Prince Vladimir had constructed upon the hill called Vydobychi and consumed the whole of it with fire." (Cross and Serbowitz-Wetzor 2012, 182-3). As was the case with their previous raids, the Cumans quickly left Kiev once they were satisfied with eh amount of plunder.

The Cumans presented a real and constant threat to all Russian principalities, yet there were some princes willing to take their chances to work with the nomad raiders. David (r. 1087-1099) was the prince of the somewhat backwater principality of Volynia, but like all Rus' princes, he desired much more. The *Primary Russian Chronicle* claimed David's ambitions earned him the scorn of Sviatopolk II and some of the other Rus' princes, who exiled him to Poland, and David responded to this treatment by forming an alliance with Bonjak and his Cuman clan in 1096. The two men then proceeded to terrorize many of the Russian principalities: "David escaped to the Polovcians, among whom Bonyak received him. The two of them advanced to attack Svyatosha in Lutsk, but made peace after they had laid siege to him in his city. Svyatosha then left his city and journeyed to his father in Chernigov. David thereupon seized Lutsk, and then departed thence to the city of Vladimir. Vasiliy the Regen immediately took to flight, so that David seized Vladimir and settled there as prince. In the following year, Svyatopolk, Vladimir, David, and Oleg won over to their cause[,] David the son of Igor', but instead of assigning him the domain of Vladimir, they appointed him to Dorogobuzh, where he died." (Cross and Serbowitz-Wetzor 2012, 197).

Although David did not succeed in taking Kiev, Chernihiv, or any other large Russian principalities, he came out of the situation relatively well, especially considering that he attempted to conquer his fellow Rus' princes. The situation did not go unnoticed by the other Rus' princes.

By the early 12th century, Cuman raids on Rus' lands were occurring often enough that the Rus' princes alternated between paying the Cumans bounties and fighting them, but even when they paid them off, it did little to stem the long-term tide of invasions and attacks. As a result, the more enterprising and farsighted of the Rus' princes realized that appealing to the Cumans' more avaricious leaders could aid them with their goals. Prince Oleg of Chernihiv (r. 1097-1115) used the Cumans in a number of campaigns against Sviatopolk II and the other Rus' princes, although he was ultimately unsuccessful (Font 2005, 270).

At the start of the 12th century, the Rus' offered a unified threat against the outside threat, and by the end of Sviatopolk II's reign, their efforts had begun to bear fruit. In 1102-1103, Sviatopolk II had gained the alliance of enough of the other Rus' princes that he was able to embark on a major offensive against the Cumans. A major Rus' army met the Cumans outside of the gates of Kiev, and this time they won the battle and drove the nomads from the region. The *Primary Russian Chronicle* explained, "The princes of Rus' and all the soldiery offered their prayers to God and made their vows to God and to the Blessed Virgin; some promised presents of food, others alms to the poor, and others supplied to the monasteries. After they had prayed thus, the Polovicans advanced, and sent Altunopa in front as a vanguard, since he was celebrated among them for his courage. The Russian princes likewise sent forward their advance party. They thus surprised the vanguard of Altunopa, upon whom they fell, slaying him and his followers. Not one of them escaped, for the Russes slew them all. The nomad troops came on like the trees of the forest, and their mass was impenetrable. The Russes straightway advanced to meet them. Now God on high inspired an awful fear in the Polovcians, so that terror and trembling beset them at the sight of the Russian forces, and they wavered. Even their steeds possessed no more swiftness of foot. But our soldiery, both foot and horse, advanced joyously to the combat. Upon beholding the effort of the Russes against them, the Polovcians fled before the Russian troops without even waiting to meet them, and our men gave chase and cut them down." (Cross and Serbowitz-Wetzor 2012, 201).

Sviatopolk II's successor, Vladimir II Monomakh (r. 1113-1125), carried on the fight against the Cumans. He scored major victories against to the Cumans in 1116 in the region of Perejaslavl, ensuring the nomadic tribe would cease to be a major problem in Russia (Font 2005, 270). The Russians would later be placed under the Mongols' yoke, but after decades of fighting with the Rus', the Cumans turned their attention farther to the south, primarily the Balkans.

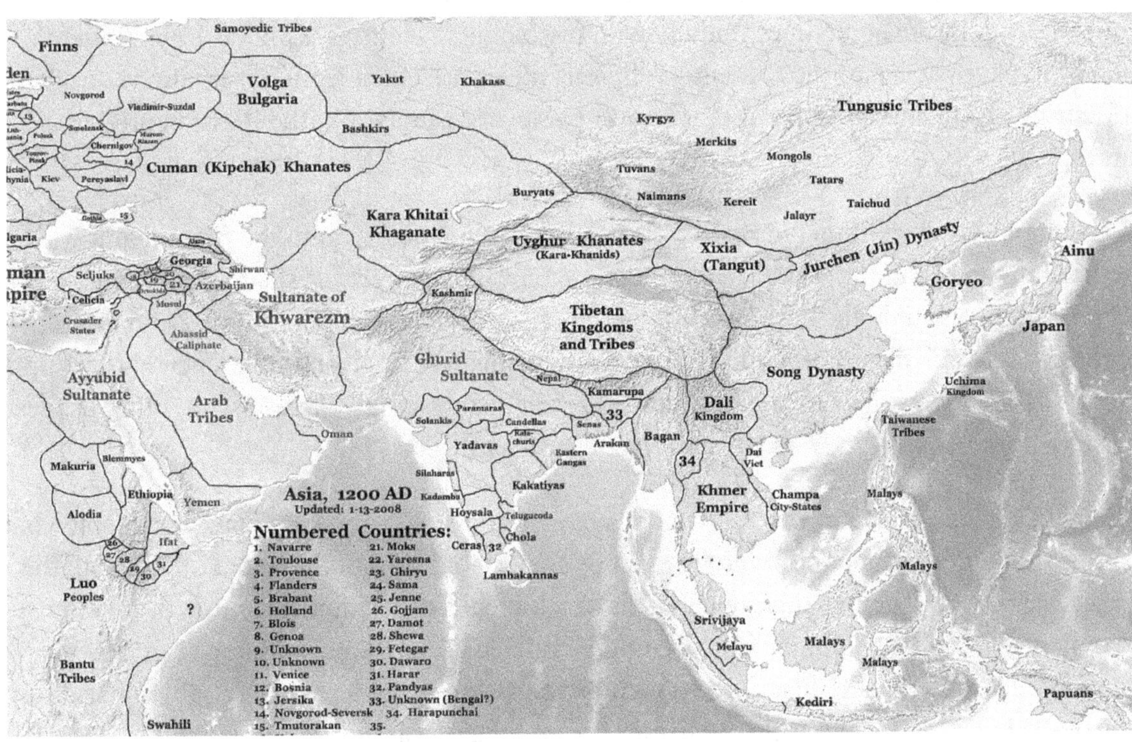

A map of the region around 1200

Cuman Culture

As enigmatic as the Cuman chronology and political history may be to historians today, constructing details about Cuman culture is even more difficult. Since the Cumans left no written records of their religious practices, academics are forced to rely on source materials by other peoples, along with studying the religious practices of other steppe peoples. The few archaeological artifacts the Cumans left for posterity were funerary goods, which aids the examinations to a certain extent. Other Cuman cultural aspects can also be gleaned from primary sources, including military tactics and political structures, which helps scholars assess where the Cumans stood in relation to other Turkic nomads, and how much they changed after their extensive contact with sedentary kingdoms across Eastern Europe.

The Cumans of the 13th century and later were almost exclusively monotheists, with most being Muslims. Monotheism was a fairly late development in Cuman culture, with the majority of the Cumans only accepting Islam sometime after they were conquered by the Mongols, while many became Christians after earlier contact with Eastern Europeans (Golden 1998, 182). Like the other Turkic nomads of the steppe, the Cumans practiced a shamanistic religion for most of their history, believing in ancestral spirits with an established pantheon, the foremost of which were the gods Coppa and Tengri (Golden 1998, 196).

Since the Cumans spent much of their lives on horseback far from cities, the elements of nature were also sacred to them. The Cumans believed that certain mountains and rivers had spiritual significance and were sometimes imbued with distinct personalities (Golden 1998, 210-14). Much of the knowledge of the Cumans' religious ideals are taken from observations of other Turkic tribes from later eras, but there are a few relevant passages in the Russian primary sources.

Warfare played an extremely important part of the Cuman culture, to the point that it was sanctified in their religion. The *Russian Primary Chronicle* noted, "Just so, even in our own day, the Polovcians maintain the customs of their ancestors in the shedding of blood and in glorifying themselves for such deeds, as well as in eating every dead or unclean thing, even hamsters and marmots. They marry their mothers-in-law and their sisters-in-law, and observe other usages of their ancestors." (Cross and Serbowitz-Wetzor 2012, 58).

The passage also indicates that the Cumans had marriage customs that may seem somewhat unconventional today, and they were viewed by the Rus' as immoral. On the other hand, the Cumans' apparently strange dietary habits have a logical explanation since they were almost certainly necessary. Life on the steppes could be difficult, and game could be scarce. If the Cuman hordes were unable to secure enough large game or plunder wealthy settlements, they had to eat whatever was available, no matter how unpleasant it may have appeared.

Shamanistic religions generally view many animals as holy or imbued with certain powers, and the Turkic nomads believed that if they knew what to look for, certain animals could auger signs or help them in battle. In his work, Ibn Fadlān wrote about how he observed many Turkic tribes revering and worshiping different animal species: "We saw a clan that worships snakes and another than worships fish and another that worships cranes. These told me that one day, while they were fighting some of their enemies and were on the point of being defeated, the cranes began to give their call behind their opponents. Their enemy was frightened and turned and fled. This is why they worship cranes." (Fadlān, 24).

The Cumans were much like the groups Fadlān observed, but they had a preference for canines. The medieval Turks believed they were descended from a primordial wolf (Golden 1998, 188), and these spiritual affinities with canines were carried on by the Cumans and noted in a passage in the *Primary Russian Chronicle*. In one passage, the Cuman chieftain Bonyak is aligned with David and about to attack an army of Hungarians: "While on their journey, they pitched a bivouac, and at midnight Bonyak arose and rode away from the troops. He straightway began to howl like a wolf, till first one and then many wolves answered him with their howls. Bonyak then returned to camp and announced to David that on the morrow they would celebrate a victory over the Hungarians." (Cross and Serbowitz-Wetzor 2012, 196). There are also documented cases where Cuman chieftains made oaths and agreements with Europeans over dead and dismembered dogs (Golden 1998, 191).

In addition to the primary sources, the Cumans left archaeological evidence of their activities behind. Since the Cumans were nomads and never built permanent settlements, most of their archaeological evidence is smaller, such as weapons, but there are a number of Cuman tombs and burials that have yielded greater finds.

The burials have uncovered two very important facets of Cuman religion. Perhaps most importantly, in the tombs for the hieftains, dogs, horses, and even humans were sacrificed and buried, apparently to ensure the chieftain had all the luxuries he needed in the afterlife (Golden 1998, 195). Furthermore, the only true example of what can be considered Cuman art, stone statues known as *kamennye baby* ("old stone women"), were frequently found near and in tombs and burials (Golden 1998, 203). It is not known for sure what these statues represented, but since many of them are women, they are not believed to have been warriors. According to medieval Persian sources, the Cumans prostrated themselves before the statues and gave them offerings, which seems to confirm their religious importance, although nothing beyond those details is known (Golden 1998, 205).

A Cuman statue from the 12th century

One of the most defining cultural features of any group, especially in the pre-modern world, is the language it spoke. As mentioned earlier, the Cumans' origins are a bit enigmatic, and what is known came from a variety of sources. That being said, it is known that they were a Turkic ethnic group and that the language they spoke, Kipchak, was in the Turkish language family. Since the Cumans controlled such a vast area, Kipchak was eventually spoken by many non-Cumans and became the *lingua franca* of Cumania by the end of the 11th century (Kara 2018, 101). Those traveling through the steppe or on the Silk Road needed to have at least a working knowledge of Kipchak in order to pass safely, which meant Christian missionaries and Venetian merchants needed to know some Kipchak, but there is little evidence the language was spoken far outside the steppes.

Perhaps the most important aspect of Cuman culture, at least in terms of their influence on the history of Eastern Europe, was their martial prowess. Like all of the peoples of the steppe, beginning with the Huns in the 5th century, warfare on horseback was central to the Cuman culture. Although texts describing Cuman raids might seemingly paint their battles as somewhat unorganized affairs, the Cumans constantly drilled their forces and were highly effective in their military endeavors. The point of Cuman raids was rarely to take land, but rather to take alienable property and leave quickly. They also made sure never to take so much booty that they would lose their quick striking and retreating abilities, which remained the keys to their success on the battlefield.

Cuman horsemen always wore light armor, allowing them an advantage over more heavily armored Rus' and other Europeans, and when the Cumans encountered a particularly staunch adversary they could not defeat in a conventional battle, they feigned a retreat (Vásáry 2004, 269). Once the enemy had broken ranks to pursue the supposed fleeing Cumans, the Cuman horsemen turned and shot arrows. A passage from the Crusader chronicle of Geoffroy de Villehardouin described this tactic in detail: "The Comte Louis came out first with his battalion. He sent back a message to the Emperor urging him to follow and immediately started off in pursuit of the Comans. Alas! how little our army kept to the course of action agreed on the night before! Instead of remaining by the camp, our men pursued the Comans for nearly two leagues, attacking them at close quarters and keeping up the chase for a very long time. At length the Comans turned round and charged them, uttering piercing yells as they let their arrows fly." (Joinville and Villehardouin, Chapter XVI, 121).

The tactic was a major reason behind the Cumans' success in war, but the tactic depended on certain conditions. The steppe, which was flat and open, was perfect for this tactic, and other locations with large plains and open fields also sufficed. Once the Cumans thrust deeper into Europe, their horseback tactics were not always as devastating, so they adapted to use a combination of diplomacy along with military tactics to gain influence in the region.

Ivan Bilibin's depiction of a Cuman camp

The Cumans in Hungary and Byzantium

There is little doubt that the Cumans had a deep impact on Russia's early history. Their constant raids eventually forced the Rus' to put their petty differences aside and unify, helping usher in the creation of a Russian nation. Although some Rus' princes took Cuman princesses as their wives, the practice was not as widespread as in other Eastern European kingdoms in later times - Rus' princes preferred to marry Rus' princesses, and if none were available, they preferred to marry princesses from other Christian kingdoms. For their part, the Cumans had exhausted their possibilities in Rus' lands by the early 12th century, so they turned their attention to southeastern Europe, where they would have a more enduring influence.

No other European kingdom was as affected by the steppe nomads as Hungary. The very name Hungary is derived from the nomadic Huns, who used the region as a base for their raids into Rome and Western Europe in antiquity, and though the Huns later dispersed and assimilated into other populations, they left such a strong influence that a large area of central Europe took their name. The modern Hungarian language and people are descended from the Magyar steppe people who entered Hungary in well-organized hordes in the 9th century, alongside a number of Cuman bands (MacArtney 1969, 51). The Cumans initially entering Hungary with the Magyar hordes were eventually assimilated into the greater Hungarian/Magyar population, but other Cuman bands remaining on the steppes continued to raid Hungary well into the 11th century (MacArtney 1969, 55).

The Magyars quickly became sedentary people, converted en masse to Roman Catholicism, and were a part of Western European civilization by the 11th century. Hungarians joined the Crusades with their German and French neighbors, and many early Hungarian kings began to see the Cumans in an increasingly negative light, especially when Cuman raids continued into the early 13th century. To counter the Cuman raids, Hungarian King Andrew II (r. 1205-1235) settled Teutonic knights in different parts of Hungary to act as buffers against the Cumans and other nomadic hordes (Vásáry 2009, 32). The Teutonic Knights helped repel the most destructive Cuman raids on Hungary and prevent worse things from happening, but they could not end the Cumans' influence on central Europe.

King Andrew II's seal

The 13th century was a time of great transition and turmoil in Eastern Europe. When the Mongols conquered the steppes in 1223, they forced what remained of the Cuman Khan to press forcibly into Eastern Europe and the Balkans. A large number of Cumans landed in the region known as Wallachia (roughly equivalent to the modern nation of Romania), where they accepted Christianity and played a major role in the formation of Hungarian, Romanian, and Bulgarian royal dynasties.

Bela IV of Hungary (r. 1206-1270) married his son Stephen to a Cuman princess, which was clearly political and intended to make the Cumans more pliant toward the kingdom. The marriage was a precedent of sorts and helped the Cumans fully integrate into European society. The Cumans marrying into the Hungarian royal family and accepting Christ were accepted by the Roman Catholic Church, and eventually the Cumans of Hungary assimilated into the greater mass of Hungary that already included Magyars, Slavs, and Germans. The Cumans' importance was recognized by the Hungarian royalty, as evidenced by the epithet by which Hungarian kings were known: King of Hungary and Cumania (MacArtney 1969, 55-56).

As the Cumans alternated between raiding the Rus' and Hungarians and fighting for them, they often looked south for more resources. South of the Danube River is the territory generally known as the Balkans, and in the 11th century, it was almost completely under the rule of the Byzantine Empire. Serbs, Croats, Bulgars, Albanians, and Greeks all lived under the hegemony of the Byzantine emperors in Constantinople, who believed that they, not the Germans and Franks to the west, were the true heirs of ancient Rome. The Byzantine forces kept the Cumans and other nomads north of the Danube for the most part until the late 11th century, but they were occasionally invited into the kingdom as mercenaries, and Cuman mercenaries played a particularly important role during the rule of the Byzantine Emperor Alexius I Comnenus (r. 1081-1118). In 1094, a former co-emperor named Nikephorous Diogenes (r. 1070-1071) employed a group of Cuman mercenaries to attack the empire and create enough chaos to allow him to regain the throne. The *Primary Russian Chronicle* noted that the plot did not work out well for Diogenes: "The Polovcians under the son of Diogenes attacked Greece, and devastated the Grecian territory. The Emperor captured the son of Diogenes and had him blinded" (Cross and Serbowitz-Wetzor 2012, 180).

A portrait of Alexius I Comnenus

Cumans would later be involved in the Byzantine military, and some would even marry into Byzantine nobility, but their focus as a group shifted once more in the late 12th century. The Cumans never made a serious effort to conquer the Byzantine Empire in the 11th century. They more than likely understood that the walls of Constantinople were virtually impregnable t that time, but the outlying areas were ripe for raiding and plundering. Still, the Cumans were not familiar with the Balkans, and its hills and mountains were not particularly conducive to their style of warfare. Thus, it's somewhat ironic that a combination of circumstances and chance encounters brought the Cumans into the Balkans, where they would have their biggest impact on European history.

The Bulgars were originally a Turkic nomadic ethnic group with many similarities to the Cumans. A group of Bulgars settled in the Balkans during the 7th century in what is today Bulgaria, and they were eventually absorbed into the local Slavic and Greek populations, accepting the Orthodox Christianity of the Byzantine Empire. After the first Bulgarian kingdom collapsed in the late 10th century, the region was once more dominated by Byzantium, but the situation did not stay static for very long. Around 1185, two Bulgar brothers named Asen and Peter fomented a rebellion against their Byzantine overlords and received the support of the Bulgar elites and the Vlakhs, who were Indo-Europeans descended from the Dacians/Romanians of the Roman Period. The Byzantine authorities quickly caught wind of the rebellion and identified its leaders, compelling Asen and Peter to flee north of the Danube River to Cuman territory (Vásáry 2009, 17). The brothers' flight to Cumania was proof of the strong relationship between the Cumans and Bulgars and marked the beginning of nearly 100 years of direct Cuman influence in the Balkans.

Asen and Peter were of partial Cuman ancestry, as indicated by the Turkic name "Asen." The two brothers apparently still had deep ties with the Cumans as well as the Vlakhs because they were able to forge alliances with both on the way to form the second Bulgarian Kingdom (Vásáry 2009, 41). Asen I (r. 1186-1196) became the first king of the new Bulgarian Kingdom, thanks in large part to the Cumans' arms.

Asen I's reign was mostly focused on fighting a war of liberation against Byzantium. The primary strategy of the Bulgarian king was to unleash the Cumans on Greek villages and cities throughout the Byzantine Empire. The Cumans' destruction was vast and unrelenting, and by 1199, they had worked their way south to Macedonia. It seemed as though nothing could stop the Cuman horde, and that the Bulgars might not only keep their independence, but also pose a serious threat to Constantinople itself. In 1202, the Bulgarians and Byzantines made peace. The Byzantine royal house was wracked with division and dissension, and in 1204 a Crusader army from the west made its way into Byzantine territory. Then, on April 12, 1204, after a series of duplicitous maneuverings within the Byzantine royal house, the Crusaders took control of Constantinople and initiated a new Latin Dynasty under the aegis of the Roman Catholic Church.

The Fourth Crusade from 1202-1204 is significant in medieval history because it was the first time a crusade was directed against another Christian group. It was also significant since it encompassed two of the four major sieges of Constantinople, and it also sparked a third in 1235 (an unsuccessful attempt to reverse the Latin gains in 1204).

Given that legacy, it's ironic that like the Crusades before it, the Fourth Crusade was originally intended as an invasion of Egypt, which had been conquered by Saladin and his uncle nearly four decades earlier. Egypt had been joined with Syria into one Muslim empire under Saladin, but it had fallen apart into two separate realms after his death shortly after the Third Crusade in 1193. Following that crusade, the main objective of the Crusaders in the 13th century was to conquer Egypt and use it as a beachhead against the Muslims in Syria who threatened Christian Palestine, a goal that should have been beneficial to all of Christendom in both the West and East.

Instead, during the Fourth Crusade, tensions between the Latin Christians of Western Europe and the Greek Christians of Constantinople came to a head after a century and three previous Crusades. This resulted in a critical breakdown of communications that resulted in an internal war within Christendom and led to the sack of Constantinople by the Crusaders. After this, the Crusaders established a Latin Kingdom in Constantinople for nearly 60 years, but it remained shaky and was eventually retaken by the Byzantine Greeks.

The Fourth Crusade was also a result of the imperialist ambitions of Pope Innocent III, one of the strongest and proudest popes of the Middle Ages, and it was a precursor of the Albigensian Crusade, the first true "internal" crusade. With that, the Latin Christians began to lose focus on the dwindling territories in Palestine, and instead Christians fell upon each other, engaging in Crusades against other Christian groups and bleeding much-needed support from the Latin kingdoms in Palestine.

The Fourth Crusade also saw the rise in power of the Byzantines' most bitter rivals in the West: the Venetians and Genoese. The Venetian Doge was later blamed for inciting the Crusaders to fall upon his Byzantine enemies, and while the situation was more complicated than that, the involvement of the Venetians in the altered direction of the Crusade cannot be denied.

Thus, even though no one realized it at the time, the Fourth Crusade was the turning point for the Crusades; after this one, the slow decline toward the Latin Christians losing the Holy Land became inevitable. Constantinople, whether as a Greek or a Latin Empire, was also fatally weakened and would eventually fall to the Ottoman Turks in 1453, long after the end of the Crusades. The Fourth Crusade would inevitably lead to the fall of the Crusader states less than a century later and also the fall of Constantinople two and a half centuries later to the Muslims. The latter would be a permanent loss to Christianity, while Christian forces would not regain control of Palestine until the 20th century.

Palma Le Jeune's painting depicting the sack of Constantinople

Speros Vryonis described the sacking of Constantinople in *Byzantium and Europe*: "The Latin soldiery subjected the greatest city in Europe to an indescribable sack. For three days they murdered, raped, looted and destroyed on a scale which even the ancient Vandals and Goths would have found unbelievable. Constantinople had become a veritable museum of ancient and Byzantine art, an emporium of such incredible wealth that the Latins were astounded at the riches they found. Though the Venetians had an appreciation for the art which they discovered (they were themselves semi-Byzantines) and saved much of it, the French and others destroyed indiscriminately, halting to refresh themselves with wine, violation of nuns, and murder of Orthodox clerics. The Crusaders vented their hatred for the Greeks most spectacularly in the desecration of the greatest Church in Christendom. They smashed the silver iconostasis, the icons and the holy books of Hagia Sophia, and seated upon the patriarchal throne a whore who sang coarse songs as they drank wine from the Church's holy vessels. The estrangement of East and West, which had proceeded over the centuries, culminated in the horrible massacre that accompanied the conquest of Constantinople. The Greeks were convinced that even the Turks, had they taken the city, would not have been as cruel as the Latin Christians. The defeat of Byzantium, already in a state of decline, accelerated political degeneration so that the Byzantines eventually became an easy prey to the Turks. The Fourth Crusade and the crusading movement generally thus resulted, ultimately, in the victory of Islam, a result which was of course the exact opposite of its original intention."

As if those results weren't bad enough, the Fourth Crusade had a major and negative effect on the crusading effort in general, especially the European attitude toward going on crusade. While the strong enthusiasm for armed pilgrimage in the 12th century had been starting to wane by the early 13th century anyway, the Fourth Crusade had the inadvertent result of doing considerable damage to both the idea and the ideal. The ideal, and the practical considerations of seeking booty and adventure, had been in balance ever since the First Crusade. However, the naked aggrandizement of the Fourth Crusade and the attack on Constantinople tipped this balance more or less permanently away from the ideal.

Furthermore, after the Crusaders took Constantinople, they found that defending it against the Byzantines, Bulgars, and Cumans was quite difficult. It did not help that the subsequent Latin dynasty in Constantinople, set up with an entirely alien and unfamiliar system to the Byzantines of foreign nobles in bonds of fealty, was too weak to take the place of the previous Byzantine Empire and defend Christianity in the East. Further, the Crusaders were extremely unpopular with their Greek subjects, who greatly resented them.

The Bulgar King Kaloyan (r. 1197-1207), known in Western sources as Johanitza, understood he had an opportunity after the Crusaders' arrival, which ultimately led to the Balkans being utterly devastated by the Cumans. Kaloyan was the king of an independent Bulgaria and Wallachia in 1205, and the remnants of the Byzantine nobility, who had moved their headquarters to the Anatolian city of Nicaea, were no longer a threat to his power. If anything, Kaloyan saw the Byzantines as potential allies who could help him gain more land in the Balkans. After all, the Kingdom of Bulgaria and the Byzantine Empire were both Orthodox Christians, and therefore, he figured, they should be allies against the Latin Christians as part of the new religious war. According to *The Crusader Chronicles*, the Byzantine nobles literally offered Kaloyan the kingdom if he helped rid them of the Westerners: "Now the Greeks, who were by nature very perfidious, still harboured thoughts of treachery in their hearts. Perceiving at that time that the French were too widely scattered over the land and too busily occupied to attend to anything outside their own particular affairs, they thought they could…easily get the better of them by underhand[ed] means. So they secretly chose envoys from all the cities in the empire and sent them to King Johanitza, regardless of the fact that he had long been their enemy and was still at war with them. These envoys told Johanitza that the Greeks proposed to make him Emperor; they would place themselves entirely in his hands, and kill all the French and Venetians in the empire." (Joinville and Villehardouin, XV, 115).

The Crusaders quickly learned that it would be much more difficult to pacify the Byzantine Empire than it was to take it. The first major point of contention was the Greek city of Adrianople, a sizable city to the west of Constantinople that both sides viewed as strategically vital. It was not the most important trading or military city in the Byzantine Empire, but it was one of the last major cities on the road to Constantinople; therefore, it was important to the strategic interests of both sides in the conflict. The Crusaders sent an army from Constantinople to take Adrianople in March 1205, but the city's inhabitants were unwilling to listen to their pleas and had no interest in joining the new Latin empire. The Crusaders put the city under siege for about a month until Kaloyan and a force of Cumans arrived, and a pitched battle took place from April 12-14. *The Crusader Chronicles* describe how the Cumans gained the advantage while the Crusaders were at Easter mass: "That night passed. In the morning, which was a Thursday in Easter Week, all the troops attended mass and then had their midday meal. The Comans came charging up to their tents; a cry was raised and everyone ran to arms, and came out of camp with battalions in proper order, according to plan." (Joinville and Villehardouin, XVI, 121).

The Crusaders then gave chase but were utterly defeated when the Cumans utilized their famed feigned retreat and turned around to deliver a devastating archery attack (Vásáry 2004, 264). Very few of the Crusaders survived the attack, and those who did were captured. The Crusaders did not embark on another campaign against Kaloyan for almost another year, which gave the Cumans plenty of time to plunder the Balkans.

The Crusaders were safe within the walls of Constantinople, but the people of the Balkans were not as lucky. *The Crusader Chronicles* portrays Kaloyan as a bloodthirsty monarch who seemed to revel in misery, using the Cumans as cudgels against the innocent Christians of the Balkans. Sure enough, the Cumans ravaged the Greek-speaking lands and threatened to besiege Constantinople: "Meanwhile King Johanitza, who was in the land with all his forces, had by this time occupied it almost entirely. The people everywhere, in the countryside, the cities, and the castles, had come over to him, and his Comans had overrun the whole territory right up to the gates of Constantinople." (Joinville and Villehardouin, Chapter XVII, 128)

In reality, the city was never in any real danger; it had never been taken by siege, and although the Cumans were familiar with siege warfare, it was not their strength. When the Cumans were unable to breach the walls, they returned to pillaging easier targets in the Balkans. Kaloyan is, once more, depicted as a ruthless marauder, but if one reads between the lines of *The Crusader Chronicles*, it had actually been a case of the king having little control over his Cuman troops. After the pillaging went on for some time, the Cumans apparently got bored and returned to Cumania: "By Whitsuntide King Johanitza had pretty well done all he wished to do in the land. But he could no longer keep his Comans together; they found it impossible to go on fighting during the hot weather, so they all went back to their own country". (Joinville and Villehardouin, XVII, 129).

Kaloyan gave the Cumans Thrace as a reward for joining his alliance, yet there was little he could do to order them to stay in the battle (Vásáry 2004, 265). The Cumans had their own commanders and leaders who, although willing to help the Bulgar king, did not apparently do so out of any great loyalty or love of Bulgaria. Cuman motivations during the Fourth Crusade were driven by the desire to acquire immediate, tangible profits.

The Greeks continued to hold Adrianople into early 1206, but the Crusaders were determined to take the city, so they sent another force to lay siege to it. If the Crusaders were to take Adrianople, it would have surely broken the Greek resistance, so Kaloyan sent a new force of several thousand Vlakh and Cuman warriors to relieve the defenders on February 1, 1206. Not only did the Vlakh-Cuman force have the Crusaders outnumbered, but they also outmaneuvered them. The heavily armored Crusaders tried to retreat to the city of Rouison but were surrounded and cut down by the more mobile Cuman horsemen. According to *The Crusader Chronicles*, "On the very night our people had set out on this expedition a large body of Comans and Wallachians, some seven thousand strong, had ridden out with the object of doing us some harm…The Comans and Wallachians, together with the Greeks of that region, came charging towards them in full force. They fell upon the rear-guard and began to attack them very savagely…The French, still fighting stoutly, had by now retreated so far that they could see the wall of Rousion only half a league away. Their opponents pressed them harder, so that the odds were too great against them; many men were wounded, as were their horses. In the end, since it is God's will that such disasters should happen, they could resist no longer and were defeated, mainly because they were heavily armed and their opponents lightly. Then the enemy began to slaughter them." (Joinville and Villehardouin, XVIII, 134-5).

The Crusaders stayed safely ensconced in Constantinople after the Battle of Rouison and never directly engaged the Cumans in another major battle, but the Cumans were not done. They moved in a southwesterly direction after the battle, leaving a large swath of destruction in their wake.

Indeed, the rest of 1206 would be a difficult year for the people of Thrace, Macedonia, and Greece. As the Crusader army remained safe behind the walls of Constantinople, it gave Kaloyan's army free reign throughout much of the former Byzantine Empire. At first, the Greeks viewed Kaloyan as an Orthodox Christian liberator, but within weeks it became clear that his Cuman horde was even worse than the Crusaders. The Crusaders may have followed false Christian teachings in their eyes, but they were still Christians, and after conquering the Byzantine Empire, the Crusaders had left the population intact for the most part, which was much better than what took place in 1206.

According to *The Crusader Chronicles*, the Cumans and their Vlakh allies went on a months-long orgy of rape, murder, and pillaging throughout Thrace and Macedonia: "Before long the Comans and Wallachians had overrun the land as far as the gates of Constantinople, where the regent, with as many men as he had at his command, was then residing. He was feeling very sad and extremely worried at not being able to get enough men to defend his land. Because of this the Comans were seizing all the cattle in the countryside, carrying off men, women, and children wherever they found them, destroying castles and cities as they passed, everywhere causing such ruin and desolation that no one has ever heard tell of anything to surpass it." (Joinville and Villehardouin, XVIII, 137).

Although *The Crusader Chronicles* were obviously biased against the Cumans like the other non-Cuman historical texts of the era, there is no reason to believe the abuses were not as bad as described. In fact, the Cumans' path of destruction was so bad that the Greeks in Kaloyan's army decided it was too much for them. Keeping a multiethnic coalition unified is no easy task, and Kaloyan seemed to have successfully done so with his Bulgarian Kingdom by appealing to the different groups' primary strengths and desires. The Cumans' primary desire was pillaging, so Kaloyan allowed his Cuman allies to pillage across the Balkans, even in Orthodox Christian territories he was supposed to protect. Eventually, the Greeks in his army and the Greeks in the cities and villages began to realize they were better off under the Crusaders: "When the Greeks who were in Johanitza's army—that is to say those who had surrendered to him and rebelled against the Franks—saw how he had destroyed their cities and their castles, and had broken every promise he had made to them, they felt they had been betrayed and gave themselves up for lost. After talking things over among themselves, they came to the conclusion that as soon as Johanitza came back to Adrianople and Demotika he would deal with them as he had dealt with other places, and if these two cities were demolished the empire would be lost to them forever. So they chose messengers in secret, and sent them to their compatriot Branas in Constantinople, imploring him to plead their cause with the Emperor's brother Henri and with the Venetians, so that they might make peace with them." (Joinville and Villehardouin, XVIII, 138).

Needless to say, Kaloyan was not happy with the turn of events, but he had to assemble a new army before he could punish the Greeks for their treachery. In the spring of 1207, just in time for Easter, Kaloyan assembled a new force and marched to Adrianople. At that point, Kaloyan was as determined to punish the Greeks as he was to take Constantinople from the Crusaders, so he organized the largest expedition to date. *The Crusader Chronicles* explained, "King Johanitza, as it happened, had already engaged a great army of Comans, who were on their way to join him; he now assembled as large a force of Wallachians and Bulgarians as he could. So much time had now gone by that we were at the beginning of Lent…Johanitza now left Wallachia with all his forces, including the great army of Comans that had come to join him, and started to invade the empire. The Comans overran the country right up to the gates of Constantinople, while the king himself laid siege to Adrianople and set up thirty great petraries around the city which hurled stones at its walls and towers." (Joinville and Villehardouin, Chapter XX, 149).

Kaloyan besieged the city for a considerable time without making any real progress. The Crusaders were able to resupply Adrianople via the sea, forcing the Bulgarian king to consider his options. His troops were limited, and he risked being outflanked by the Greeks, the Crusaders, or both, but before he could make a decision, the Cumans made it for him. As they had done before, the Cumans simply grew bored of the campaign and left. According to *The Crusader Chronicles*, "However, since all events are ordered by God's will, it so happened that the Comans, whom Johanitza had sent out to overrun the land, declared, on their return to camp with all their spoils, that they did not intend to remain any longer in his army, but would go back to their own country. So they parted from Johanitza, and since, without their help, he did not dare remain before Adrianople he withdrew his forces and left." (Joinville and Villehardouin, XX, 153).

The Cumans did not play a major role in the Fourth Crusade after that point on the battlefield, but they made their presence felt once more with another important action. After the failed siege of Adrianople in 1207, most of the Cumans returned to their land north of the Danube, but their inability to take Adrianople should not be viewed as a battlefield loss or failure. Although it is true that siege warfare was not the Cumans' strength, they had successfully laid siege to other cities before Adrianople, and they had brought some cities down after 1207. Modern historians who have examined the Balkans during the Middle Ages have theorized that the Cumans' retreat to Cumania after Adrianople had more to do with goals and expectations than with the failure of the Cuman military. The Cumans were driven, for the most part, by a desire to plunder, and they had no long-term goals to acquire more land (Vásáry 2004, 269). The region of the steppe they controlled was more than enough for their type of lifestyle and social structure, which meant conquering the sedentary Balkans would have complicated their relatively simple system. The Cumans had no desire to rule over a subject population - if they wanted slaves and riches, they would take them, and if they needed food, they would either herd, hunt, or trade for it.

Not all of the Cumans retreated north of the Danube in 1207, and it appears that at least a few made one last statement in the Fourth Crusade. Although most of the Cuman horde left Bulgaria, Kaloyan continued to employ Cumans as his elite guard. It was the job of these Cumans to protect the king as well as fight in the army, but Kaloyan was murdered sometime after the failed siege at Adrianople in 1207. Most modern scholars believe that it was probably his Cuman bodyguards who committed the act, since the assassins would have had access to the king (Vásáry 2009, 53). The details of the assassination remain unclear, and it is not known with certainty that Kaloyan's Cuman bodyguards were the ones who killed him.

That said, Vásáry believed they had a motive. In light of the atrocities Kaloyan had perpetrated on the Balkans, it is more than likely the killers were paid to rid the world of the vicious tyrant. The Cumans were no more or less vicious than other people of the period, so it is difficult to believe that Kaloyan's bodyguards would have turned on him for no reason, or even over a personal affront. The most likely explanation is that either the Greeks or Crusaders had bribed one or more of the Cumans to commit the murder.

Alternatively, the assassination might have come from within the Bulgarian royal house. Kaloyan's successor was his nephew, Boril (r. 1207-1218), who was never viewed as legitimate by many Bulgars. To placate his critics, Boril married Kaloyan's Cuman wife and entered into a rapprochement with the Hungarians and Byzantines (Vásáry 2009, 57-61).

The Cumans were no longer the terror of southeastern Europe during Boril's rule, but more and more of them filtered into the region due to a much larger and temporarily unstable force spreading west across the steppe.

The Cumans and the Mongols

In antiquity and the Middle Ages, mass migrations often produced a domino effect, as could be found during the latter stages of the Roman Empire and in Eastern Europe. Beginning in the 10th century, the Magyars pushed their way into Europe before landing in Hungary. Then, after becoming sedentary people, they founded a kingdom in that country. They were followed (and often pushed) by the Cumans, who played the role of kingmaker and helped establish a kingdom in Bulgaria before they were pushed further west into Europe.

The group responsible for moving the Cumans was the strongest and most notorious of all the nomadic hordes: the Mongols. Although the Cumans and Mongols shared a similar nomadic, steppe culture, the Mongols wanted to add Cumania to their khanate in the early 13th century, and they were not willing to negotiate.

The emergence of the Mongol horde meant that old enemies quickly became allies. The Cumans formed an alliance with Kiev and some of the other Rus' states to oppose the Mongols. After a series of minor encounters, the Rus-Cuman Army met the Mongol horde near the Sea of Azov in 1223. The Mongols attacked the Cuman trading settlement of Sudaq, causing great destruction, as they often did wherever they went (Vásáry 1988, 263). The Rus-Cuman Army then organized and rode out to meet the Mongol horde near the Kalka River. The ensuing battle was devastating for both the Rus' and the Cumans.

Mongol armies besieged Rus cities in 1236-1237, initially demanding tribute from the Kievan Rus rulers to no avail. The Mongols, however, took Crimea in 1238 and Kiev in 1240, laying waste to the once rich and densely inhabited capital before moving further east into Europe.

After the Battle of Kalka, the Rus' states were essentially under the suzerainty of the Mongols for the next 200 years, forced to pay yearly tribute. The Cumans, however, were much harder to defeat due to their nomadic nature. The Cumans continued to give the Mongols organized resistance on the steppe until 1241, when most of the Cuman leadership and many of the Cuman people were absorbed by the Mongols and various Eastern European peoples (Vásáry 2009, 9).

The Mongols were pushed out of the region by the Poles and Lithuanians, who then occupied state territories in the 14th century. Poland seized areas in the west, known as Galicia, while Lithuania occupied a northern area called Volynia. The Mongol-Tatars, however, retained control of the Crimean Peninsula, using it as a base for trade, including that of slaves, with the Ottoman Empire. The Tatars would actually strengthen their grip on the Crimea after the Golden Horde's demise and continue terrifying other European powers. By allying themselves with the Ottomans, the Tatars seemingly lost the potent position they had when they were a part of the Mongol Empire, they were still close to being a superpower from Southeast Europe and the Middle East. Meanwhile, the Ottomans would continue to expand their territory and threaten other European nations for centuries to come.

Russia also began expanding its influence by playing a role in defeating the Mongol hordes. The Russian ruler, Grand Prince of Moscow Ivan III, married the final heir to the Byzantine throne, Sophia (born Zoe) Palaiologina, the daughter of the last emperor of Byzantium, in 1480. Sophia would go on to be the grandmother of Ivan the Terrible, the first tsar of Imperial Russia from 1547-84. As a result of this lineage, the Romanov tsars would claim they were the torchbearers of Orthodox Christianity, descending directly from Byzantium.

The Byzantine Empire was in sharp decline by the 15th century. Constantinople fell to the Ottomans in 1453, effectively ending the empire, although it limped on for a few more years before finally disappearing.

Meanwhile, the Cumans would be forced to make their final migrations, setting up their evolution from nomads to a sedentary society.

Cuman Integration

Although the Cumans lost control of Cumania to the Mongols, many of them stayed to become part of the Mongol Golden Horde. Most of these Cuman-Mongols lived in Crimea, where they later became valuable assets as tax collectors for the Mongols in the 13th and 14th centuries (Vásáry 1988, 262).

As much as they served as mercenaries for the Bulgarian Kingdom in the early 13th century, according to Byzantine sources, they often served as the Mongols' regional muscle in the latter decades of the century. If Crimean tribute payments were not promptly made, the Mongols sent the Cumans either to get payment or to send a very violent message.

It is believed that the Cumans brought the Black Death to Europe when they besieged the city of Kaffa, a productive city of merchants and artisans from Europe and Asia, in 1347. When the leaders of the city refused to pay the Mongols, the Cumans surrounded the city and began catapulting body parts of people who had died from the plague over the walls (Jotischky and Hull 2005, 120). When the Cumans gained entrance into Kaffa, they unleashed the most devastating biological weapon in world history on Europe.

The Mongols may have brought the "state" of Cumania to an end (if it can rightfully be classified as a state), but the traditional Cuman culture had already been in decline for quite some time. Throughout history, whenever nomadic and sedentary cultures developed extensive contacts and relations, the nomadic culture usually adapted the traits of the sedentary culture, if it was not outright assimilated into it. The Cumans' predecessor in Hungary, the Magyars, were one such example, but other examples can be found throughout history on nearly every continent. Nomadic cultures often had the upper hand militarily early on in confrontations, but after a while, the nomadic people began to covet their sedentary neighbors' lifestyle, and the Cumans were no different in this respect. As noted earlier, the Cuman elite began to marry into Eastern European nobility in the 11th century and accepting many of their traditions, including Christianity.

The Cumans gave up their shamanistic religious beliefs fairly quickly after the Mongol conquest, and the religion the Cumans had accepted in the 13th century was largely the result of where they were assimilated into the local population (Golden 1998, 218). The Crimean Cumans became a target of conversion for the Roman Catholic Church. Although Crimea is closer to Constantinople, Catholic missionaries followed Venetian and other Western merchants to the region where they converted a fair amount of Cumans. Ibn Battuta, the Islamic geographer, visited Crimea in the early 14th century and noted that Cumans (Kifjak) were still Christians. He wrote, "Leaving this place I proceeded by sea for the city of El Kiram (Crim), but suffered considerable distress in the voyage, and was very near being drowned. We arrived, however, at length, at the port of El Kirash, which belongs to the desert country of Kifjak. This desert is green and productive: it has, however, neither tree, mountain, hill, nor wood in it. The inhabitants burn dung. They travel over this desert upon a cart they call Araba. The journey is one of six months; the extent of three of which belongs to the Sultan Mohammed Uzbek Khan; that of three ore to the infidels. I hired one of these carts for my journey from the port of Kirash to the city of El Kafa, which belongs to Mohammed Uzbek. The greater part of the inhabitants are Christians, living under his protection." (Battuta, XII, 74-75).

The Mongols were fairly tolerant in terms of religious freedom for the first 100 years or so of their rule, but as the hordes became decentralized and adopted Islam, they began enforcing aspects of Sharia law on their subjects, and Crimea became increasingly hostile to Christians until all Christian missionaries in the region left after 1342 (Vásáry 1988, 271). After that, the remaining Crimean Cumans assimilated with local Mongol and Turkish populations and adopted Islam.

The initial Mongol onslaught into Cumania created a mass Cuman migration into the Balkans in 1237. The Cumans were familiar with the Balkans by that time, having served in the Bulgarian Kingdom's armies in great numbers and in lesser numbers for Byzantium.

A number of the Cuman elite welcomed this influx, but when another wave entered the region in 1241, the sheer number of them caused problems (Vásáry 2009, 64-65). Most of the second wave of Cumans came from Hungary in the north, which was also under duress from the Mongol horde. Eventually, after engaging in another pillaging campaign, most of the Cumans who had entered the Balkans in the 13th century settled down and became Christians. The Cuman elite, which was already tied to the Bulgar elite, continued to marry with the nobility of the region and eventually helped to found three royal dynasties in Bulgaria and one in what is now Romania (Vásáry 2009, 166).

Some of these 13th-century Cuman refugees also looked to what was left of the Byzantine Empire for a new home. The Greeks restored their dynasty and pushed the Crusaders out of Constantinople in 1261, although the once great city was a shadow of its former self. Besides suffering from internal conflicts that often resulted in assassinations and attempted coups, Byzantine land was constantly threatened by Turkish tribes. The Byzantine emperors did not have enough native support to field an army large enough to protect their interests, and they were forced to turn to some of the very people who threatened their borders. The destruction wrought by the Cumans on the Byzantine Empire in the early 13th century served as a sort of resume for their employment by the Byzantine emperors in the following decades. Although Cumans had already served in the Byzantine military and the Greeks were familiar with them due to their raids and trading with them, a large wave of the nomads entered Byzantine land after they were defeated by the Mongols. Most continued on to Bulgaria, Serbia, and what would become Romania, but those who stayed on Byzantine land served in the emperor's armies until the late 13th century (Vásáry 2009, 114-15). Thus, the Cumans quickly assimilated into the larger Greek population and later faced the Ottomans, beginning in the 14th century.

It is nearly impossible to put a number on how many Cumans entered Europe, converted to Christianity and were assimilated after 1237. It is estimated that 40,000 Cumans entered Bulgaria in 1241 (Vásáry 2009, 65), and since there were other waves of Cuman migrants into Eastern Europe before and after that date, the overall numbers were probably in the hundreds of thousands. Just as many Cumans elected to stay in either Crimea or on the steppe, joining the Mongol horde in the process. Since Cuman and Mongol culture was similar, the ethnic lines between the groups were blurred, but with steppe people, the clan was always the most important group identity. Cumans married into the most powerful Mongol clans, and the importance of the clans gradually diminished.

Few armies could withstand the Cuman raids or the Mongols, but neither of these nomadic groups could overcome Islam's proselytizing power. Islamic states based in Persia sent waves of missionaries to the Volga region to convert the heathen horsemen, beginning in the 13th century. Muslim merchants and Sufis were the vanguards of the conversion effort, which, by the late 13th century, had begun to bear fruit (Golden 1998, 225-6). By the late 14th century, Islam had become the Mongols' official religion. The Islamic identity eventually replaced the clan, the most important group identity within the Mongol Empire, which served to further assimilate the Cumans into the greater mass (Kara 2018, 102).

Elements of Cuman culture continued well into recent centuries. For example, the Cuman language continued to be spoken in Hungary, and long after the Cumans were assimilated into the greater Hungarian population, Cuman ancestry was still a source of pride for many people. As Magyar was the official language of the Hungarian Kingdom and the language spoken by an overwhelming number in the population, Cuman became a novelty language that eventually died in the 18th century (MacArtney 1969, 57). Once the Hungarian nobility had merged with the Habsburg royal house to form Austria-Hungary in 1867, most people had all but forgotten Hungary's Cuman connection.

Online Resources

Other books about Russian history by Charles River Editors

Other books about the Cumans on Amazon

Further Reading

Battuta, Ibn. 2004. *The Travels of Ibn Battuta in the Near East, Asia, and Africa: 1325-1354.*Translated by Samuel Lee. Mineola, New York: Dover.

Cross, Samuel Hazzard, and Olgerd P. Serbowitz-Wetzor, eds. and trans. 2012. *The Russian Primary Chronicle: Laurentian Text.* Cambridge, Massachusetts: The MediaevalAcademy of America.

Fadlān, Ibn. 2012. *Ibn Fadlān and the Land of Darkness: Arab Travellers in the Far North.* Translated by Paul Lunde and Caroline Stone. London: Penguin.

Font, Márta. 2005. "Old-Russian Principalities and Their Nomadic Neighbours: Stereotypes of Chronicles and Diplomatic Practice of the Princes." *Acta Orientalia Academiae Scientiarum Hengaricae* 58: 267-276

Golden, Peter B. 1998. "Religion among the Qipčaqs of Medieval Eurasia." *Central Asiatic Journal* 42: 180-237.

Joinville, Jean de, and Geoffroy de Villehardouin. 1963. *Chronicles of the Crusades.* Translatedby M. R. B. Shaw. London: Penguin.

Jotischky, Andrew and Caroline Hull. 2005. *The Penguin Historical Atlas of the Medieval World*. London: Penguin.

Kara, Dávid Somfai. 2018. "The Formation of Modern Turkic 'Ethnic' Groups in Central and Inner Asia." *Hungarian Historical Review* 7: 98-110.

Klyashtornyj, Sergej G. 2005. "The Polovcian Problem (II): Qipčaqs, Comans, and Polovcians." *Acta Orientalia Academiae Scientiarium Hungaricae* 58: 243-248.

MacArtney, C. A. 1969. "The Eastern Auxiliaries of the Magyars." *Journal of the Royal Asiatic Society of Great Britain and Ireland* 1: 49-58.

Vásáry, István. 2009. *Cumans and Tatars: Oriental Military in the Pre-Ottoman Balkans, 11851365*. Cambridge: Cambridge University Press.

———. 2004. "Cuman Warriors in the Fight of Byzantium with the Latins." *Acta Orientalia Academiae Scientiarum Hungaricae* 57: 263-270.

———1988. "Orthodox Christian Qumans and Tatars of the Crimea in the 13th-14thCenturies." *Central Asiatic Journal* 32: 260-271.

Free Books by Charles River Editors

We have brand new titles available for free most days of the week. To see which of our titles are currently free, click on this link.

Discounted Books by Charles River Editors

We have titles at a discount price of just 99 cents everyday. To see which of our titles are currently 99 cents, click on this link.